I'm thinking...travel!
JOURNAL

▲▲▲

I'm thinking...travel! JOURNAL

Copyright © 2018 by Cate Brubaker, Thinking Travel Press

All rights reserved. No part of this publication may be reproduced, distributed, or transmitted in any form or by any means, including by photocopying, recording, or other electronic or mechanical methods, without the prior written permission of the publisher, except in the case of brief quotations embodied in critical reviews and certain other noncommercial uses permitted by copyright law.

ISBN: 978-1727595345 (Thinking Travel Press)

For more information or bulk sales requests, please visit www.thinkingtravel.com to contact the author directly.

THIS JOURNAL BELONGS TO:

_____

TRAVEL DATES:

_____

DESTINATION(S):

_____

▲▲▲

Hello, Traveler!

For tips on how to make the most of your travel journal, visit us at:

www.thinkingtravel.com

Happy travels!

We are happy to partner with Wanderful, an international community of diverse women travelers around the world.

Meet other travelers in your destination or connect with like-minded women at home with an online membership community, 50+ local chapters, a woman-to-woman homesharing network and more.

By purchasing this journal, you get one month to try us completely free! Learn more at http://community.sheswanderful.com

before travel

PACKING LIST

ITINERARY

-
-
-
-
-
-
-
-
-
-
-
-
-
-
-
-
-
-
-
-
-
-
-
-
-

HOW I FEEL ABOUT MY UPCOMING TRAVELS

WHAT I MOST WANT TO ACCOMPLISH ABROAD

WHAT I'M LOOKING FORWARD TO ↑

↓ WHAT I'M NERVOUS ABOUT

WHAT I WANT TO DO, TRY & EXPERIENCE ABROAD

-
-
-
-
-
-
-
-
-
-
-
-
-
-
-
-
-
-
-
-

"To tavel is to live."
– Hans Christian Andersen

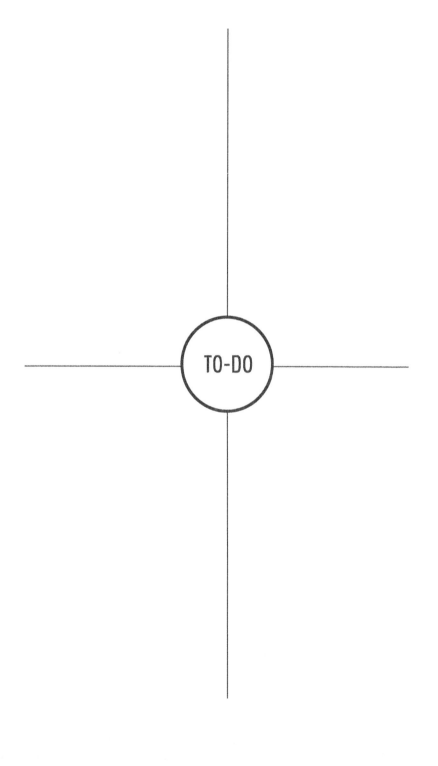

NOTES

during travel

JOURNALING PROMPTS

Make a list of...
- Today's top 3 moments
- What I ate and drank today
- What I hear, see, and smell right now
- How I keep busy on planes/trains/buses
- What I'm reading/listening to/eating/drinking
- Words I've learned in the local language
- How much things cost (coffee, toothpaste, etc)
- Cultural questions and observations
- What am I grateful for on this trip

Jot down a few lines describing...
- My very first impressions
- What I'm feeling today
- Music I've recently heard
- Conversations I've overheard
- My daily schedule
- What public transportation is like
- The best food/drinks/sweet treats I've tried
- How people dress
- Animals I (don't) see
- Who I met today

Write a few paragraphs about...
- What I'm learning about myself
- How I'm growing and changing
- Something that was initially hard or scary for me
- Advice I'd give pre-trip me
- How my expectations have met up with reality
- What I'm observing/reflecting on/inspired to do
- What I'm remembering/planning/dreaming about
- How I feel about "home"

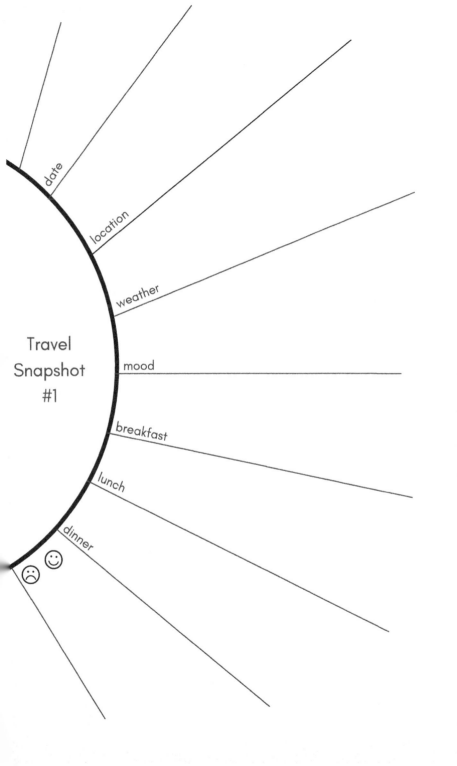

date place

date   place

"Take only memories, leave only footprints."
- Chief Seattle

date						place

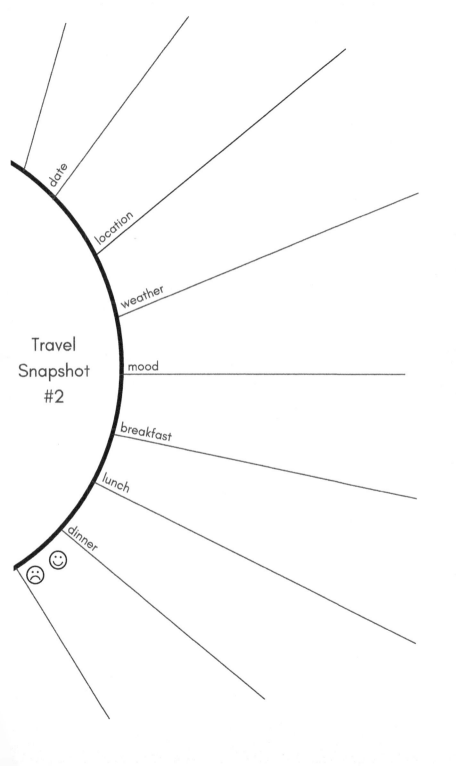

date　　　　　　　　place

date   place

"Live life with no excuses, travel with no regret."
- Oscar Wilde

date place

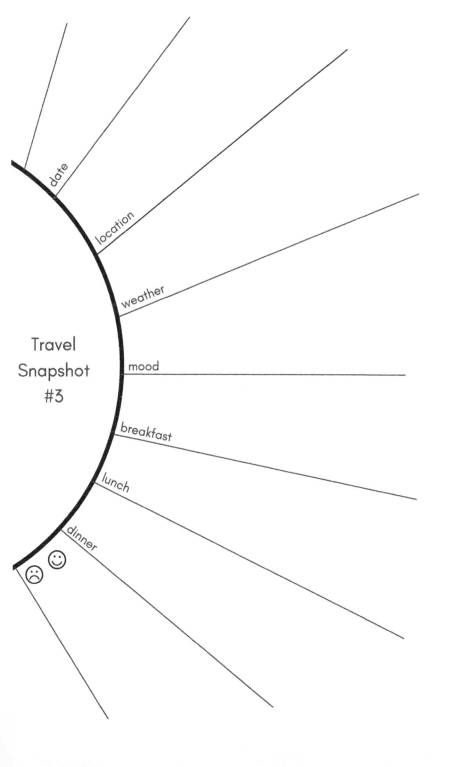

_____
date   place

dateplace

"We travel not to escape life, but for life not to escape us."

– Anonymous

date   place

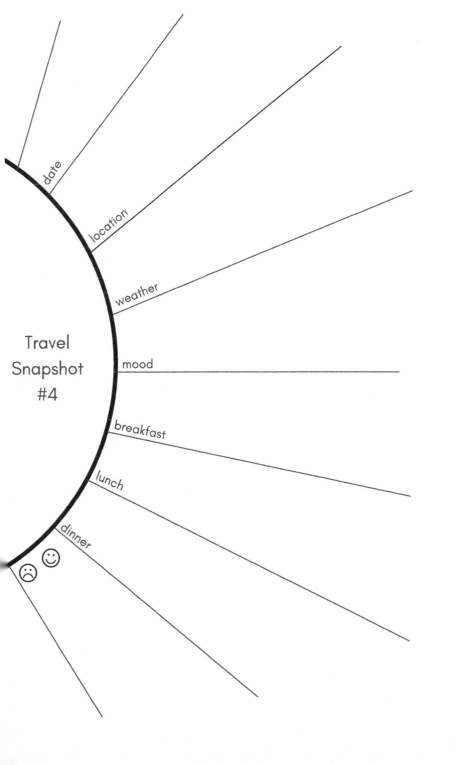

date   place

date   place

> "A person susceptible to 'wanderlust' is not so much addicted to movement as committed to transformation."
> ~ Pico Iyer

_____

date   place

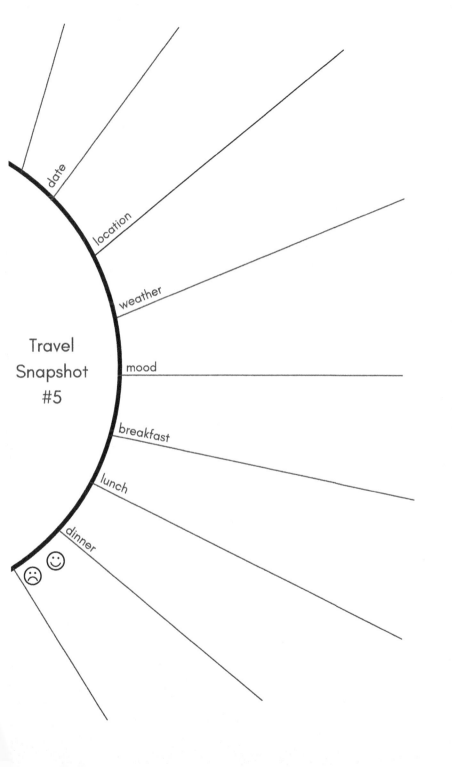

date　　　　　　　　place

_____
        date   place

"I'm in love with cities I've never been to and people I've never met."

– John Green

_____
   date   place

after travel

WHAT I'M GLAD I PACKED	WHAT I WISH I'D LEFT BEHIND

BEST TRAVEL MOMENTS

WORST TRAVEL MOMENTS

↑ WHAT I LEARNED ABROAD

↓ WHAT I STILL WANT TO LEARN

WHAT I LOVE (AND MISS) ABOUT BEING ABROAD ↑
↓ HOW I CAN INTEGRATE ABROAD INTO HOME

FUTURE TRAVEL IDEAS

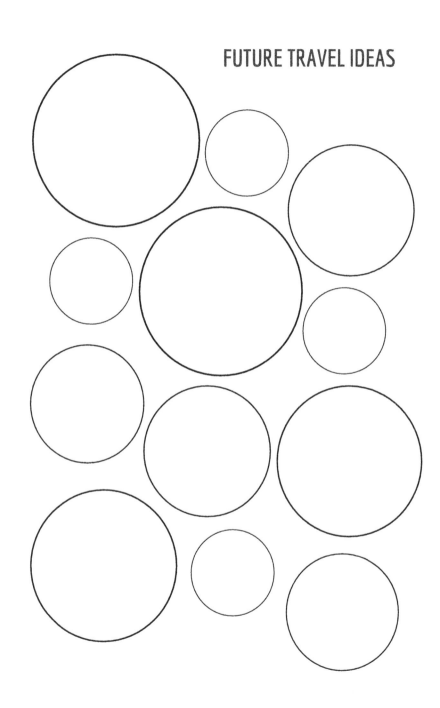

BACKYARD ADVENTURE IDEAS

HOW I LIKED FEELING ABROAD

HOW I CAN FEEL THAT WAY AT HOME

WHAT I LIKE ABOUT WHO I AM WHEN ABROAD

HOW I CAN BE THAT WAY AT HOME

FOR MY
NEXT TRIP...

NOTES

"Travel isn't always pretty.
It isn't always comfortable.
Sometimes it hurts,
it even breaks your heart. But that's okay.

*The journey changes you;
it should change you.*

It leaves marks on your memory,
on your consciousness, on your heart,
and on your body.
You take something with you.

Hopefully, you leave
something good behind."

– Anthony Bourdain

▲▲▲

I'm thinking...travel! JOURNAL

MY NEXT DESTINATION:

_____

Time to order another travel journal!

Made in the USA
Monee, IL
22 January 2020